fierce LOYALTY

Unlocking the DNA of Wildly Successful Communities

D1304388

Sarah Robinson

Published by Hayfield Publishing
Birmingham, Alabama
Copyright ©2012 Sarah Robinson
All rights reserved.

Design and composition by Lori Paquette
Cover design by Lori Paquette

Library of Congress Control Number: 2012947883

ISBN: 978-0-9882458-0-8

ATTENTION CORPORATIONS, UNIVERSITIES, COLLEGES AND PROFESSIONAL ORGANIZATIONS: Quantity discounts are available on bulk purchases of this book for educational, gift purposes, or as premiums for increasing magazine subscriptions or renewals. Special books or book excerpts can also be created to fit specific needs. For information, please contact Hayfield Publishing, 1919 Oxmoor Rd. Suite 374, Birmingham, AL 35209, (317) 426-6143.

For David, Thomas, and Nicholas.

You've taught me the meaning
of Fierce Loyalty.

table of contents:

foreword

The honest truth? It's not hard to throw a business together and make money. Just find something people want or need, and sell it to them for more than it costs. Result? Success—financial success, at any rate.

Companies like Microsoft, Walmart, Verizon and any bank you want to name are all evidence that not only can this be done, you can in fact make very large sums of money following just this formula.

But what if that's not your only goal? What if you don't want to just extract money from an anonymous bunch of customers? What if you want to make a difference in the world, by producing products or services that people love—that they can't get enough of—that they rave about to their friends and colleagues, that they proselytize, evangelize, obsess about? What if—gulp—you actually *care* about what you're doing?

Other companies—global organizations like Apple, Whole Foods, Patagonia, Harley Davidson, Motley Fool, and thousands of smaller businesses like Hiut Denim and Valve Software—have shown that there is another way—that you can be financially successful (extremely so, if you wish) while at the same time not just satisfying your customers needs—but actually thrilling them.

Why don't all organizations do this? Why do so many businesses settle for 'meh' when they could have 'wow!'? The reason is simple—it's hard work. Building Fierce Loyalty doesn't happen just by chance—it's the direct result of making difficult choices. Building raving fans means choosing a path that is unmarked and little taken—a path that's hard to follow, and which seems at times to be leading you right over a cliff.

Eschewing compromise, committing to quality, remaining transparent, encouraging dialog—these are all things that frankly, are easier to do without. You *can* build a business without them, and your life will be easier—but the result will be something bland, unremarkable and ultimately unsatisfying.

The good news is that if you're one of those people who truly want to make a difference—and if you're reading this foreword I suspect you are—then achieving your goal of building a remarkable organization (and keeping it that way) just got a whole lot easier.

Sarah Robinson knows what Fierce Loyalty is, and how to build it. She has spent her life transforming the ordinary into extraordinary. In organizations large and small, in for-profits and not-for-profits, Sarah has worked to expunge mediocrity by consistently raising the bar—not just for herself, but for those she works with. And along the way she has uncovered the patterns of building Fierce Loyalty—patterns that lie hidden in plain sight, patterns that are buried under the mundanity of running a business.

Now in this book, you have in your hands a road map to the extraordinary—a GPS for attaining the remarkable. For the first time, Sarah has laid out the specific steps and crucial decision points that you will face in building an organization that doesn't just transact with people—any organization can do that—but one which truly transforms them.

Take this model and apply it to your business. You will make a difference in the world, and your Fiercely Loyal customers will thank you.

– Les McKeown
Wall Street Journal bestselling author of
Predictable Success and *The Synergist*

introduction

**Everything I Needed to Know
about Community, I Learned
from a College Dorm**

My first job out of college was at St. Louis University (Go Billikens!), where I was hired as a "Community Development Coordinator" in the residence hall system. (In retrospect, this was a prescient title. All of my work since that first job, whether in a corporation, a political campaign, a non-profit, or with my small business clients, really boils down to coordinating and developing community.)

I was so excited. This job was right up my alley. As an undergraduate, I'd started organizations and worked in a residence hall, so I quickly jumped on the idea of strengthening a student community.

After just a few days on the job, though, I realized there were a few unanticipated challenges in making this whole community development thing work:

Challenge #1 – Most of the students who lived in my residence hall lived in the St. Louis area. They viewed their dorm room as simply a convenient place to sleep, not as a "home away from home." They had no need for community.

Challenge #2 – The physical building of this particular residence hall was old and worn. It suffered from poor lighting, outdated bathrooms, small rooms, and no common space—not the ideal physical environment for creating a warm and inviting community.

Challenge #3 – Like all residence hall programs, ours operated on a very lean budget. We had to make the right choices on how to spend the little we had.

Challenge #4 – I was young, fresh out of college, with no real idea of what I was doing. (Mercifully, this challenge became a huge asset because I didn't know enough to know what an uphill battle I was fighting.)

As often happens in the midst of growing and building things of value, the challenges that loomed in front of me felt insurmountable at times. As you begin thinking about your community, similar challenges may come to light for you as well.

Challenges like:

- How on earth are we going to find, much less connect, such a far-flung group of people?

- What are we going to talk about once we run out of our standard marketing messages?

- How do we draw a group together and foster a true feeling of community that sticks?

I learned one very important lesson as I took on the challenges of my first job. It's a lesson that will help you face your own challenges as you build Fierce Loyalty. Once you grasp it, you'll use it again and again and it will propel you forward no matter what stands in your path.

That lesson was and is: make a decision. Every day, decide that a fiercely loyal community is your goal, no matter what.

For two years, I made the decision each day to build a community out of college students. More important, I made the decision to believe that my efforts were worth it. Worth the frustration, worth the long hours, worth the mistakes, worth it all. And bit by bit, day by day, I watched my students embrace the idea of building a community in their dorm. They developed a sense of pride about where they lived. They learned to trust each other and the housing staff. They felt a passionate sense of loyalty to their community.

This didn't happen overnight. It took six months before I saw any signs of progress. A group of students who lived in my dorm decided they wanted to do something to bring residents together. They asked me if they could revive a special Spirit Night at a St. Louis University home basketball game. Prior to tip-off, we reserved a room so that all the dorm residents could eat together. Each floor competed in a Team Cheer competition. Special buses transported everyone to the game, and all the students sat together in a specially designated section of the arena.

As I looked around at this group of residents laughing, talking, engaging and cheering together, I knew that the kind of community I envisioned was beginning to take hold. And the next morning, I had my proof as students showed up in my office to make sure Spirit Night became an annual event.

Over time, I watched as dorm residents continued working together and building deeper, stronger relationships, stepping up to the challenge of learning new leadership skills, and collaborating on wildly successful community-building projects. All of these outcomes evolved in spite of the daunting challenges I mentioned earlier.

In fact, by the end of my two-year commitment at St. Louis University, the students were so invested in the well-being of their community that they sent a representative to interview the candidates for my replacement to ensure that person would be a good "fit." Experiencing this kind of return on my investment of time and energy hooked me on the idea of building communities for the rest of my professional life.

I started thinking about why community was possible under these less than ideal circumstances. As I pulled apart the strategies I'd used at St. Louis University, it hit me: I'd uncovered the essential elements needed to build and foster a Fiercely Loyal community. Of course, I didn't use that label—or even realize at the time that I had discovered anything noteworthy—I just called it a job well done.

My colleagues, however, did take note. They watched as I created a tight-knit community out of "nothing" and affectionately called this ability, "The Midas Touch."

While getting compliments is a wonderful thing, here's one of the most important things I've learned after building community after community over the past twenty years: There is no "Midas Touch." There is no "One Big

Secret." There is no one precise path to a fiercely loyal community. There is only what I call DNA—the critical building blocks that must be in place for Fierce Loyalty to form.

Combining the knowledge I gained at St. Louis University, my community building experience from the past twenty years, and my research into the inner workings of wildly successful communities, I've discovered that this DNA boils down to five building blocks:

1} A Captivating Common Interest
I found a galvanizing common interest that inspired residence hall students and pulled them toward the community.

2} People Who Share this Common Interest
I identified students who shared this common interest, knowing they were my very best candidates for forming and leading a community.

3} A Set of Compelling Needs
I listened to what students needed on several levels instead of telling them what they needed. You have no idea how novel this approach was in a college residence hall.

4} A Specific Organizational Structure
I built a very loose but specific environment to meet those needs and kept my eye on where I wanted the community to go as I built it.

5} Advanced Evolution of the Community:

I knew that with the right parts in place, and with the right kind of nurturing, the most critical and long-lasting pieces of a Fiercely Loyal community would take root, grow, and evolve.

This DNA is not unique to the community I built at St. Louis University. It exists within *every* wildly successful community I've built or researched, whether it's a community around a brand, a non profit, a cause, a political campaign, or a Neighborhood Watch.

And it gives these stand-out communities the kind of raving fans, customers, clients, supporters or members every organization dreams of having—the kind whose support never wavers, whose evangelism is contagious, and whose investment in the success of the organization is legendary.

In the coming pages, you'll learn the building blocks inside this DNA and start applying them to your community—whether you are in the early planning stages or have a community that you know could be stronger. Together, we'll walk through planning, building, and accelerating your community and make Fierce Loyalty an integral part of your business model and your organization.

Turn the page and let's get going!

part one

The ROI* of a Fiercely Loyal Community

"Community" is a very hot marketing word right now. Most organizations and companies are scrambling to make sense of this latest and greatest trend. Many even have a "Community Manager" on their organizational chart—a huge step in the right direction. Too often, though, I see businesses that are trying to build a community, but don't have an integrated strategy for making it a vital part of the company's operation.

And really it's no wonder. So much conflicting and confusing information about community is swirling around out there, it's hard to get a clear picture of what a community is and why having one is so critical in this new economy. Without clear definitions and meaningful ROI, making decisions and building strategy around community can be difficult, bewildering, and even feel like a wasted effort.

Until now.

*Until recently, ROI, or Return on Investment, was strictly an accounting term, used to quantify the cash value of the return on an investment. Today, it has a much broader definition and is used to describe cash value and other important, non-cash, returns on investment.

Let's Start With What Community Is...

To have a conversation about Fierce Loyalty and how to unlock the DNA of wildly successful communities, it helps to talk about community in very specific terms. Understanding what it is and why it is important is crucial to any organization that wants to thrive in today's marketplace.

So that we have a common understanding about exactly what a community is, I consulted the Merriam-Webster online dictionary. I discovered a very rich and nuanced definition that goes something like this:

*A Community is a **unified** body of individuals, such as:*

a. the people with **common interests** living in a particular area; for example: "the problems of a large community"

b. an **interacting** population of various kinds of individuals in a common location

c. a group of people with a common characteristic or interest **living together** within a larger society; for example, "a community of retired persons"

d. a body of persons or nations having a **common history** or common social, economic, and political interests; for example, "the international community"

e. **a body of persons of common and especially professional interests scattered through a larger society;** for example, "the academic community"

While most corporations and organizations are primarily focusing on definition (e) *a body of persons of common and especially professional interests scattered through a larger society*, there are such incredibly relevant tidbits in the other four definitions that I would like to tease them out and use them to raise the grain on how we think about community.

- *"Unified"*—That the group is unified is an almost assumed part of the definition—a given. The definition of "unified" is "acting as one." When you look at the community you are building, would you say they are acting as one?

- "People with *a common interest*"—Having a common interest is the frame that holds a community together. Does your community have a common interest? (*Note:* This common interest may or may not be specifically about your brand.)

- "An *interacting* population"—Members of a thriving community interact and engage with each other. Do yours?

- "A group of people...*living together*"—While I'm not suggesting community members move in together, I do want to point out that the online world is not the exclusive domain for communities. The strongest, most successful communities combine online and offline connection points.

- "A body of persons or nations having a *common history…*"—Do not under estimate the power a common history can give to a community and to fostering Fierce Loyalty. Are you giving your community experiences that build a common history with you and with each other?

The Case for Community

With those traits pointing the way for *what* we're trying to develop when we talk about community, we turn our focus to *why* we should actually have one (other than "it's the latest and greatest, and every other organization has one.")

A robust, active community brings distinct business advantages to the table—advantages that set you apart from the competition. Because I've been building and fostering communities in some form or fashion since 1986, I've experienced first hand the power of these ROIs again and again, no matter what the type, size, or goals of the organization.

Here are my 5 favorites:

- *Empowered Evangelists*
- *A Grassroots Research and Development Team*
- *A Hungry Client Base*
- *Reduced Client Attrition*
- *Happier Clients*

Now let's look more closely at each of these:

Empowered Evangelists

When members of your community become invested in what you and your organization are up to in the world, they feel like they are part of the team and become invested in your success. And because they want to be a part of this success, they start spreading the word. They also relish the chance to look like "cool kids" to their friends. They get the inside skinny. Maybe they get to test your widget, or maybe they get to be the really cool in-the-know-early-adopters. And they want to tell their friends about this awesome new thing!

I see lots of businesses try to create a community for this sole purpose: a free marketing department, if you will. While it's understandable that businesses want all the help they can get around marketing, I've never see this strategy end well.

The more successful strategy is creating a singular focus for people to gather or rally around your organization. Give them ownership; empower them; treat them as a vital part of what you are up to. Find out what matters to them (which may have nothing to do with your core business, by the way) and deliver it. An invested heart is the greatest marketing asset in the world.

case study snapshot:
Hands on Memphis
(now called Volunteer MidSouth)
www.volunteermidsouth.org

When I moved to Memphis, Tennessee in 1993, I helped breathe life into what was then a fledgling non-profit called Hands On Memphis (HOM). This organization was perfect for me. I was single, I was new in town, I didn't know anybody and I was looking for a way to productively fill my time. Hands On Memphis fit the bill.

The premise behind HOM was simple: volunteering should be easy, it should be fun, and it should be social. In my early days as a volunteer, I spent as much time working on projects as I did planning and organizing social events for volunteers. Our theory was that people who socialized together would encourage each other to volunteer more—and more often—because they would be volunteering with people they knew.

We also knew that if we made volunteering fun, cool, and hip, word would spread. We were right. Volunteers brought friends to help with projects as often as they brought friends to our parties. Either way, the new people had so much fun that they just kept coming back— often with friends of their own.

In a time when community volunteering was at an all time low, especially among those under the age of 65, Hands on Memphis knocked out 20 volunteer projects a week in our early days. Now, more than 100 projects are completed every week, transforming the City of Memphis with the power of a Fiercely Loyal community of volunteers.

All because we broke from the traditional approach to volunteering and created a reason for raving fans to spread the word.

A Grassroots Research and Development Team

We learned in Marketing 101 that we are supposed to ask those in our "niche" what solutions they want before we go and create them. But here's the thing about that. As Henry Ford once said, "If I had asked people what they wanted, they would have said faster horses."

If you have a group of people who are deeply connected to you and your brand, who are as committed to it as you are, you can do more than just ask them what they want. You can talk with them and empower them to help you tease out the REAL problem they need a solution for. You can tap into their imaginations. You can give them stuff you've thought up so they can test it and give you feedback.

I've built R&D into every community I've ever developed. I bring an idea, hand it over to the community, and then watch what they do with it. From universities, to political campaigns, to businesses, tapping into this knowledge and creativity, and fostering a collaborative environment, builds a better mousetrap every single time.

More importantly, this approach helps me understand the community members better: how they think, what they like, what they hate, and what they are really looking for. All of these insights make me more connected while teaching me how to deliver better and more meaningful solutions.

case study snapshot:
St. Louis University

www.slu.edu

When I was charged with building a residence hall community at **St. Louis University**, I had Hall Councils—councils made up of members of each floor. I wanted students to be heavily invested in their own success, so I did something radical. Instead of dictating what the dorm rules had to be, I asked the hall councils to figure out what kind of rules they wanted to have. I gave them boundaries and parameters, of course, but then I let them design the rules, how they would be enforced, and what would happen if they were broken.

I knew I was taking a huge risk, but the students took the ball and ran with it, giving rise to a community spirit and pride that surprised even me. They hammered out hall agreements. They posted rules on hall bulletin boards. They laid out the procedure for rule infractions. They rose to the challenge beautifully.

I remember standing in the stairwell one night, listening to a sophomore girl stand down two boys who were running through the halls making a game out of breaking ceiling fixtures. She heard them coming and stood her ground when they got to her floor. She wasn't about to pay for broken fixtures, so the boys could leave or get turned in. And quickly her other floormates joined her, effectively backing the boys right out of the hall.

Over time, this kind of unified self-responsibility became the way the entire dorm operated. Students took ownership of the kind of community they wanted to live in, and they took responsibility for creating and maintaining it.

In fact, they took so much ownership that, when I left, they sent delegates to my boss demanding to be included in the interview process for my replacement. They knew that my successor could make or break the community they now saw as their own.

> All because I included them in researching, testing, developing and owning their vision of a community rather than imposing my vision on them.

◎

A Hungry Client Base

In the end, a business needs people who are willing to trade money for their "thing," right? If customers and clients are involved in developing the "thing" from idea to offer, they will line up to buy it when it's finally ready. Even if they haven't been that involved, a thriving community of loyal fans who are invested in what you are about in the world will count on the fact that you've created something awesome just for them. That's what they trust you to do.

Again, some businesses build a community for the sole purpose of selling something. These same companies are surprised when it doesn't work out. No one likes to be sold to. And no community built for that purpose is going to last very long.

Instead, invest in the care and feeding of your community long before it's time to bring anything to market. Learn about the people showing up. Talk to them. Invite them to be a part of some of things you are up to. (If this sounds little—or a lot—like dating, it is. The way you start and build a community is almost identical to the way you start and build a relationship.)

They will feel connected to you and will like the fact that you and your organization "get" them. When you do bring something new to market, they'll be waiting on the edge of their seats to buy it.

case study snapshot:
Samuel Adams

www.samueladams.com

Samuel Adams recently concluded a "Crowd-Craft Project" held on its Facebook page which was designed to craft a new brew for the Sam Adams label. Participants weighed in on all aspects of the beer including color, clarity, body, malt, hops, and yeast. (And by the way, you had to be a "Fan" of their Facebook page in order to participate.)

Once all the votes were in, Samuel Adams set about brewing the collaborative recipe. Now they could have stopped there and just capitalized on the R & D value of their community. But because they are so smart, they made a wise, strategic choice. They partnered with marketing genius and former Apple exec Guy Kawasaki and debuted this new beer at his famous South by Southwest Party in Austin, Texas. The beer was also on tap at bars all around Austin during this annual event that many consider Mecca for the social media crowd.

Here's what is so exceptional about their approach: Samuel Adams debuted a beer, crowd-crafted on social media, at a social media mega-event. And because they created a community that encouraged members to share their opinion and got them invested in making a collaborative brew, they had a community of customers waiting on the edge of their seats for that beer to be available for purchase.

Reduced Client Attrition

We all know that it costs much more to obtain a new client than it does to keep an old one, right?

So let's think about this: Your competition offers a similar widget at a similar price. Maybe a few more, or a few less, bells and whistles. Sometimes they beat you on price. Sometimes you beat them on customer service. To your clients, you both look about the same. Sometimes they order from you. Sometimes they order from them. Attrition is high and retention is low.

To stay profitable, you have to go out and beat the bushes for new clients month after month because of customer and/or order fall-off. It's an expensive strategy in terms of both money and manpower.

Now let's envision this scenario with a thriving community built around your company or your widget. Your clients feel a part of and contribute to this community. It connects them to each other, it values their input, and it makes them happy. They can't imagine not being a part of it.

When it comes time to make a buying decision, they don't even consider buying from anyone but you. Why? Because buying from you keeps them connected to this community that they love.

case study snapshot:
Harley Davidson
www.harley-davidson.com

Harley Davidson is one of my all time favorite examples of Fierce Loyalty. They are the standard bearers because they get it. They understand exactly how to encourage and foster a community of stark-raving fans.

Harley communities have existed for forever. Harley Davidson Corporate chooses to harness these communities, supporting—helping, and promoting them—rather than trying to control them from the top down. They understand that one of the biggest reasons people ride a Harley is because they value their freedom to be an individual.

They understand this so well that right on their corporate home page it says: *"The refusal to conform both sets us apart and unites us."*

Dig further into their site and you'll see that Harley Davidson Corporate is deeply focused on serving Harley communities and the riders who are in them. There is an official Harley Owners Group (H.O.G) that riders can join. (Having a small barrier to entry makes a community even stronger.) Once they are members, they can join locally run chapters, organize or attend local or national Harley events, finance the purchase of a new or used (even privately owned) Harley, insure their Harley, find rider groups specifically tailored to their interests, plan a ride, check out rides planned by others, and the list goes on and on and on.

With this kind of attention, it's easy to understand the legendary loyalty Harley owners feel for both their community and their bikes. They can't imagine what life would be like without either of them. If anything, God forbid, should ever happen to their bike, it won't even enter their heads to consider replacing it with another brand. Why? Because if they rode anything other than a Harley, it would mean giving up the community they are so deeply invested in. And that simply isn't going to happen.

Happier Clients

Isn't that why we are in business—to make clients happy?

When customers and clients are happy, we are inspired to do better work, and our vision for what we can accomplish expands. Happy clients complain less, refer more, and often spend more money. And happy clients are just more fun to do business with.

So how does a community foster happy clients?

According to the copious research done lately on the science of what makes us happy (much of that research is housed here: http://www.authentichappiness.sas.upenn.edu), scientists have discovered that, more than wealth, more than the pursuit of pleasure, it is engagement and connection that makes us feel happiest and most fulfilled.

What this research means for us is that there are prospects and customers out there who are actually looking for ways to engage, connect and have conversations. And here's the really interesting part: they want to engage in this conversation with you and your company, *and* they want to engage with each other.

By creating and fostering a community that provides these connection points, you are offering community members the very happiness ingredients they crave. And when prospects and clients begin to view your organization as a source of happiness and fulfillment, it will be much, much harder for them to leave you.

case study snapshot:
Running Room
www.runningroom.com

Running Room could be just another store that sells stuff runners want. Lots of stores do that and are quite profitable. But Running Room, a successful chain of Canadian stores, decided to be much, much more than that.

With terrific insight into what their customers (and potential customers) really want, Running Room created both online and offline gathering places for anyone interested in running or walking. If you never buy a thing, you can gather at a store for a live clinic, find running buddies, join a running club, start and end your run, or peruse the list of running events they keep meticulously up-to-date.

They've also created an online gathering place that does many of the things listed above plus offers online forums to talk to other runners, extensive gear guides, and a vast resource list. They've even included a "giving" section that allows community members to make charitable donations, sponsor runners, or get involved in a Running Room sponsored event.

Running Room knows that loyalty is built on much more than a pair of shoes. It's built on happy customers who belong to a community that connects runners to the running world and to one another. And judging by the growth of this privately owned company, fostering this kind of connection and engagement is very good for business.

Takeaways and Action Steps for ROI

In the end, the ROI on a thriving, well-run community boils down to this: happier, more engaged clients and customers. And because community members feel great about being engaged with you, they will invest more of their resources with you. Depending on the focus of your organization, this could mean higher, more sustained sales, referrals, and recommendations, or donations and volunteer hours.

If you decide you want some of these bottom-line benefits, here are your first action steps. Whether you are a beginner at all of this or have experience under your belt, taking these three steps will give you more clarity and more insight so that you can make a bigger impact with the community you are creating.

◎ **Review your reasons for wanting a community.** And if your answer is "Because xyz company has one," or "My boss read that every company has to have one," or "It's another channel to push out sales information," hit pause and dig deeper to uncover the real reasons your organization is pursuing a community and the benefits of actively building one.

Building a community, especially a fiercely loyal one, requires a significant commitment. To sustain that commitment, you and your team must be crystal clear on why you are doing what you are doing every day.

Revisit the five categories of ROI we just discussed. Which one would have the biggest impact on your business as it stands today? Which one is the most likely one to aim for first? Which excites you the most?

Pay attention to your answers and you'll discover your reason.

◉ **Decide how you will know your community is a success.** If you're thinking that the number of members will be your success metric, expand your vision. Numbers are actually the least important thing you can measure.

The key to determining success is to first decide what your business goal is for the community. Increased sales? Increased brand loyalty? More word-of-mouth recommendations? More volunteers? Reduced client attrition? Developing a new widget? Knowing what you want your community to do for your business is a critical decision to make before you embark, even if that choice evolves along the way.

Once your community is active, you can look at factors such as engagement, conversions, interaction, feedback, etc., through the lens of that goal.

◎ **Determine where the resources and the staff to support your community will come from.** If your answer is "the intern will handle it" or "somebody in our marketing department knows all that," think bigger. While interns and the marketing department have skill and knowledge to contribute, a successful community depends upon an integrated strategy, meaning that people from all levels and from all departments are involved and invested in its success.

And if you are a one person shop without levels and departments, success is absolutely possible for you. Determine the resources you have available to dedicate to your community. How much time can you allocate? What resources and relationships do you already have that you can use to build a community? What resources and relationships do you need to get in place?

The point here isn't to develop a huge project plan but to be intentional on the front end about how you envision your community coming together.

BONUS TAKEAWAY: *Never, ever forget that it's not about your organization. It's about the community and the people in it.*

part two

**Unlocking the DNA of a Thriving,
Fiercely Loyal Community**

If the ROI of a Fiercely Loyal community is so compelling, why doesn't every organization have one?

Many leaders I talk to believe that developing a community of rabidly loyal fans is often a matter of luck or an alignment of stars, where everything just seems to come together. Of course there are certain elements everyone knows must be present, like trust, pride, and solid communication. But without a model to illustrate when and how these and other key elements come together effectively, the "it either happens or it doesn't" mindset can take hold, stymieing efforts to create a Fiercely Loyal community.

As I began working with my clients to put community at the center of their businesses, I realized how few models were out there that gave clear directions they could follow and a visual picture they could grasp. So I built one. I dissected the thriving corporate, non-profit and small business communities I've helped build and I dug into the inner workings of some of the most loyal communities out there. My research pointed to one thing. The DNA I'd discovered and used at St. Louis University was the same DNA shared by each and every organization I'd researched.

When we unlock this DNA, we find simple, clear building blocks that anyone can use to develop a Fiercely

---

Loyal community. No more guessing. No more hoping. No more wondering if you're going to get it right.

Introducing The Fierce Loyalty Model

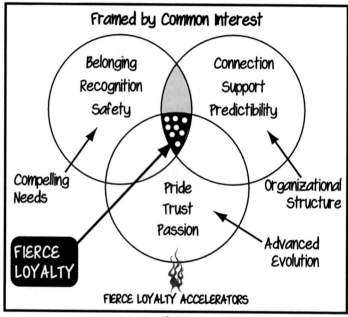

(fig. 1)

The drawing above is a model of the Fierce Loyalty DNA (fig. 1). I'm going to break it apart and give you a brief introduction to each building block and then show you how to turn up the heat on accelerating the growth process. The important thing to understand in this moment is that Fierce Loyalty evolves holistically—everything works simultaneously and together over time. If any piece is missing, the entire model collapses.

Many organizations have a few of these building blocks in place. Some even have most of them, which demonstrates a huge commitment to building a community. These organizations are driven because they know that they're on to something. Yet they often feel frustrated because they aren't seeing the success they know is possible.

The model I'm about to unpack guides you past that frustration and shows you how to put the right pieces in the right places so that you can create a Fiercely Loyal community— the one you see at the very center of the diagram. The organizations I talk to who've done the work to reach Fierce Loyalty feel the palpable hum of a wildly successful community, complete with all the bottom-line benefits we talked about in Part 1.

Unlocking Fierce Loyalty

There are five building blocks that come together to form the DNA of Fierce Loyalty:

1. **A Captivating Common Interest**

2. **People Who Share this Common Interest**

3. **A Set of Compelling Needs**

4. **A Specific Organizational Structure**

5. **Advanced Evolution**

Understanding the Captivating Common Interest and the People Who Share It: Getting a firm handle on the first two building blocks is the crucial initial step in creating Fierce Loyalty. This work isn't as sexy as the heart of the model so it's tempting to skip it. Don't do that. Without a strong foundation to support the remaining building blocks, the rest of the model—and your results—will fall apart.

Building Block #1: A Captivating Common Interest

(fig. 2)

When I was at Saint Louis University, figuring out how to knit together groups of diverse and seemingly disparate students into a fully-functioning community, I knew I needed something captivating and inspiring to anchor the building process. Something that would support all the necessary pieces and help them hold together while the community grew. I needed a frame.

I kept asking myself, "What does every single student in the residence hall want that is strong enough to hold a community together?" I realized that the students themselves might know, so I asked the student-run hall council. Their immediate reply: "We want you to treat us like we're responsible adults who can manage our own affairs." In that spilt second, I got what I needed. I knew that the common interest of being treated like responsible adults could galvanize an entire community. I'd found my frame.

After discovering the idea of using a frame to anchor and inspire a thriving, high-functioning community of students at St. Louis University, I've used this concept as the starting point for the other communities I've brought together. For a group of small business owners, I initially posed a frame of "running a successful business with better, smarter strategies". The business owners themselves re-set the frame to "running a successful business with better, smarter strategies that feel aligned with who I am." When bringing a community together for a political campaign, we set a frame of "Better representation that gives us a better future" to draw like-minded people together. And when a community spontaneously formed around a fundraiser led by my nine-year old, I thought the common interest was the cause he was helping. After watching and listening to his supporters, I discovered that the common interest frame was "believing in a nine-year old's passion project enough to help him succeed."

In studying many other wildly successful communities, I found that they, too, have discovered that a captivating common interest "frame" holds all the elements of Fierce Loyalty together and sustains them as community develops and evolves.

The frame you use for your community can be very specific, such as an interest in Samuel Adams beer. Or it can be much more general, such as an interest in hand-crafted beers. For example, if your company sells organic dog food, the common interest might be in the pet lifestyle your product specifically affords. Or it may be about a bigger subject that is connected to your product, like a passion for holistic pet care, which encompasses several specific interests.

Takeaways and Action Steps For Building Block #1

◎ Think about some of your favorite brands that have strong communities. Can you identify the common interests that serve as frames for these communities? If you've followed them for a while, have you watched the frame shift in any way? Are they using a broader bigger frame that encompasses several specific interests or a frame of one specific common interest?

◎ Brainstorm your frame. There are individuals, even groups of individuals, who have an interest in (a) your product or service, (b) an idea connected to your product or service, or (c) both.

Brainstorm a list of all possible ancillary interests, causes, and ideas that could have a connection to your business, and choose two or three that make the most sense and feel the most captivating. (If your list isn't particularly captivating or inspirational, keep digging at the core interest until you hit on something that is.) It's okay to pick one frame and then find out you need to modify it.

Building Block #2: People Who Share This Common Interest

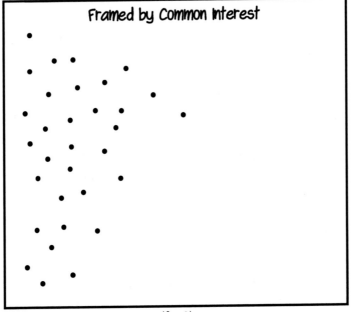

(fig. 3)

Once you establish your frame, you'll discover a wide variety of people inside it who share your defined common interest (fig. 3). Some of these people might know each other, and sometimes they've even formed small groups. But often these individuals are not connected in any way and the small groups that do exist don't interact with each other.

When we started Hands On Memphis, we began with a frame/common interest of "Making a Difference in Our City in a Way That Is Easy, Fun, and Social." The people we initially saw inside that frame looked a lot like us: young, single professionals who wanted to make a difference and have fun doing it. This made our job really simple because we knew exactly how to find those people.

As time went on, however, we discovered a whole bunch of other people inside that frame that we'd never even considered. People like HR directors looking for a way to encourage corporate volunteering, college students who wanted to volunteer without a long-term commitment, families who wanted to volunteer together in a high impact way. By looking beyond our original, assumed demographic, we found these individuals who, along with the young, single professionals we'd originally identified, gave us a huge pool of people who might be interested in building the volunteer community we envisioned.

I cannot over-emphasize the importance of these first two elements and the foundation they set: the frame, and the people inside the frame. Spend adequate time fully exploring and defining your community frame and the people who are or can be a part of it. Being fully grounded in the first two building blocks will inspire all your efforts. Plus, you'll save time, money, and endless frustration. I've seen many communities crash and burn because these foundational underpinnings were weak or non-existent.

Takeaways and Action Steps For Building Block #2:

◎ **Find the people inside your frame.** Now that you've brainstormed ideas for your own frame, it's time to locate the people having conversations about the common interests on your list. Conversations are happening all the time, online and offline, and there's a really good chance that the topics on the list you made are part of these conversations. Your job is to find them.

When I worked on a political campaign for a candidate running against a long time incumbent, we had to build a community from scratch. The entire campaign team and I networked everywhere (this was before the days of websites and Facebook). We went to business events, homeowner association meetings, informal social gatherings—anywhere we knew people were gathered and talking about what was happening in our city. Using this grassroots approach of going where the conversations were already happening, we built our entire volunteer campaign organization.

To find relevant conversations online, do a Google search for blogs and set up Google alerts for your best keywords. Do a keyword search on Twitter. Tweetdeck and other Twitter clients allow you to set up a column based on a specific keyword so you can monitor conversations on an on-going basis. Conduct similar searches on Facebook and LinkedIn.

In addition to your online search, read the business section of your local paper and look for meetings around a topic that is connected to your business or organization. Uncover where face-to-face conversations are already taking place and take part in them. Online conversation is awesome, but nothing can take the place of real, face-to-face connections.

◎ **Listen more than you talk.** Once you find a few relevant conversations, observe them and get to know the participants before rushing in to talk. Engage when you can contribute or be helpful rather than hijack the conversation, turning it into a marketing pitch.

When Hands On Memphis first began, we focused solely on reaching young, single professionals. When people outside this demographic started showing up at our projects, we had no idea how they heard about us. So we listened. Several groups of people said "Yeah, a co-worker told us about this project so our department decided we'd all volunteer together today." (An implicit need expressed by corporate workers.) Then we heard families say "Our next door neighbor told us about this project and we've been looking for a way to volunteer as a family." (An explicit need expressed by families.)

Because we focused on listening, we discovered a much bigger group of people interested in "Making a Difference in Our City in a Way That Is Easy, Fun and Social." And we began to understand exactly what motivated them to actively engage with our work and with our community.

Once the first two building blocks are in place and your foundation is set, it's time to focus on the heart of the Fierce Loyalty model. Each of the following three building blocks are important and helpful in their own right. But only when all three are fully engaged, does a collection of fans and followers develop into a powerful community movement supporting your mission, services, or products.

Building Block #3: Compelling Needs

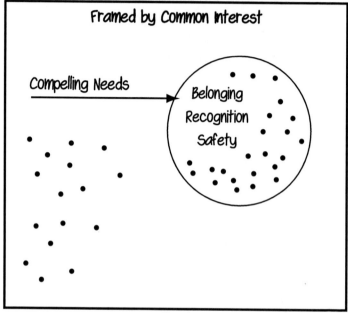

(fig. 4)

Within the broad group of people who populate your frame, you'll find individuals who are great candidates for your community and individuals who are not. Just because they share the common interest doesn't necessarily mean they want to be part of your community.

As we grew the community for Hands On Memphis, we met lots of people who loved what we did and we loved them, and yet our community wasn't the right fit for them for myriad reasons. And that was okay. Actually, it was more than okay. It was exactly as it was supposed to be.

As we move through the rest of the Fierce Loyalty building blocks, these insights will become clearer and more useful. The important thing to grasp now is that you can recognize your best candidates because they "raise their hands" and distinguish themselves because they have three very specific needs (fig. 4):

~ **The Need for Belonging**. They want to be a part of something bigger than themselves.

~ **The Need for Recognition**. They want to be seen, heard, and acknowledged.

~ **The Need for Safety**. They want to feel secure among like-minded people.

If you're thinking these sound a bit like a portion of Maslow's Hierarchy of Needs, you're right. Most human beings have an internal drive to fill some basic emotional needs. Remember the happiness research I mentioned earlier? We crave a sense of connection and engagement because it makes us feel truly happy. It's natural that we seek out opportunities that will fill these cravings.

My blog, Escaping Mediocrity (http://www.escaping-mediocrity.com), began as a way to articulate my personal mission and vision. Incredibly fed up with the status quo I found in my personal and professional life, I wanted a place to express my voice. I felt the deep need for belonging, recognition, and safety as I worked through finding my own path to work and to live in a fulfilling way.

case study snapshot:
SURFRIDER Foundation
www.surfrider.org

In 1984, history teacher and Ventura, CA surfer, Glen Hening, and a small group of fellow surfers co-founded The Surfrider Foundation because they needed a formal way to protest threats to their local surf break at Malibu Point. These founders shared a common passion for surfing and common concerns about surfers getting sick from the polluted runoff and the environmental threats from rapid coastal development. Converting this passion and concern into their personal mission and vision, Glen and his friends organized themselves quickly and scored their first victory at Malibu just a few short weeks after officially forming.

Inspired by this early success and by the unity they saw at the 1984 Olympics in Los Angeles, this small group felt certain that there were other surfers in California, the US, and around the world who were passionate about their sport and concerned about protecting their beaches and favorite surfing spots. So they set about establishing local chapters and appealing to those surfers who shared their vision and who wanted to be part of something that made a difference (belonging), who wanted a vehicle for having their voices heard (recognition) and who wanted the safety and comfort of doing this challenging work with a group of like-minded people (safety).

From small and humble beginnings, the Surfrider Foundation has grown into an organization with over 50,000 members and 90 chapters worldwide. Embracing their common mission of "the protection and enjoyment of oceans, waves, and beaches through a powerful activist network," these members and chapters work at a grassroots level cleaning beaches, monitoring water quality, providing educational programs, lobbying congress, and much more.

As a coach and a business strategist, I'd been a part of the online business world long enough to know that there was a handful of people expressing similar feelings and needs. The same-old, same-old way of doing things was beginning to chafe them and they, too, yearned for a place to gather with like-minded adventurers to forge a new path.

Armed with this knowledge, I launched Escaping Mediocrity. I wrote about my own hopes and fears. I wrote about things that no one else was saying out loud. I wrote about my vision for creating a community where people could feel fully self-expressed, warts and all.

In short, I created a beacon to guide those with needs similar to mine so that they could find safe haven at Escaping Mediocrity. Here, they discovered a place to belong, a place where their voices were heard and valued and a place safe enough to say whatever needed saying. By fulfilling my own needs and, at the same time, fulfilling the needs I'd heard from others, the Escaping Mediocrity community quickly became an online "home" for adventurous entrepreneurs who are determined to forge their own path.

Takeaways and Action Steps for Building Block #3:

◎ **Listen.** Listening is a recurring theme on the path to creating Fierce Loyalty. As you observe and contribute to conversations in and around your frame, you'll hear your ideal community candidates express their needs for Belonging, Recognition and Safety. These needs may be overtly expressed, like my candidates for Escaping Mediocrity, or more subtly implied, like the surfers who make up Surfrider.

◎ **Stay out of the convincing business**. You will find people inside your frame of common interest who are not ideal candidates for your community. Don't try to convince them to join. They won't be happy and, in the end, you won't either. At Hands

On Memphis, we talked to people everyday who loved the idea of volunteering that was easy, fun and social, but they didn't have the needs of Belonging, Recognition and Safety. Rather than try to convince them to join us anyway, we let them go so we could focus our attention on those who had a need for a community like ours.

◎ **Ask for referrals and recommendations.** If you've found a handful of perfect community candidates, ask them who else they know who might be interested in joining. Most people hang out with others who are a lot like themselves. Tap into these connections online by making it easy to share, re-post or re-tweet about your community. Offline, ask people to bring friends to the next community gathering.

Building Block #4: A Specific Organizational Structure

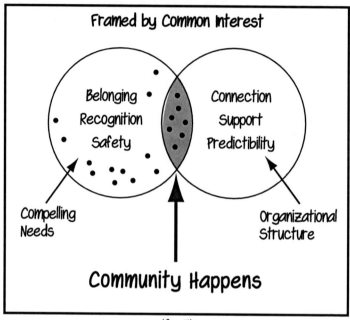

Framed by Common Interest

Belonging
Recognition
Safety

Connection
Support
Predictibility

Compelling Needs

Organizational Structure

Community Happens

(fig. 5)

The people in your developing community—those people *inside* your frame who 1) share a common interest and 2) need Belonging, Recognition and Safety—are looking for ways to get these needs met. Their hunt may be conscious or subconscious, but the drive to find a community with a structure that can deliver is the same (fig. 5). Their search ends when one of two things happens:

- These people find each other, organize themselves and create their own structure for a community (like the Occupy Wall Street Movement).

OR

- An outside organization provides the community structure and they find their way to it (like Weight Watchers).

Who creates the structure isn't nearly as important as getting the structure right. This is the place where many organizations struggle unnecessarily. They are unsure of the "what's and the how's" of a successful community, so they spend a great deal of time spinning their wheels. My own work and my research show three specific structural "must-haves":

~ **A Structure For Connection**. Community members want to connect with your organization and with each other. These vital connections are the basis for strong communication and relationships. Connection points can be online and include social media channels, a blog, a membership site, etc. or they can be offline and include small, informal gatherings or large events. The best communities incorporate both online and offline connection points.

~ **A Structure For Support**. Community members want support from your organization and they want to give and get it from other members. This support can happen through the connection points above, and is enhanced by sharing resources, answering questions, problem-solving, online and/or offline support meetings, etc. Successful communities build in specific mechanisms that make it easy to get and give support.

- **A Structure For Predictability**. Community members want to know that their community operates in a predictable way. This includes knowing when, where, and how the community will gather, communicate, and function. Thriving communities know that this kind of certainty comes through clear communication, predictable processes, gathering times, and operations.

When an organization offers a community that includes Connection, Support and Predictability, those individuals who are looking for Belonging, Recognition and Safety will beat a path to its door.

When I originally launched Escaping Mediocrity, I put a structure in place that matched my personal vision and mission. I posted on a predictable schedule, connected with everyone who left a comment, and offered support wherever I could. (I also bolstered the predictability and the safety factor by setting the ground rule of "no flaming attacks or I will block and ban the offender.")

As the community grew, the members built on my structure and took an ownership stake in how the community functioned (which I highly encouraged). I marveled at how my personal mission and vision began to morph into a new and better mission and vision created and owned by the community as a whole.

For the Surfrider Foundation, creating a community out of the far-flung surfing population meant forming and empowering local chapters all over the United States and around the world. These local chapters connect environmentally-minded surfers with each other and the larger Surfrider organization, provide a mechanism for supporting local efforts and the Surfrider mission, and give much needed predictability to the local and global operation. By empowering each local chapter to act independently, Surfrider allows them to develop their own missions and their own visions that fit with the overall mission and vision of the Foundation.

case study snapshot:
Ikea Hackers
www.ikeahackers.net

Begun in 2006 by a woman in Malaysia who uses the pseudonym Jules, Ikea Hackers is a blog community of global Ikea enthusiasts who post their furniture "hacks," or design modifications, not for pay or because Ikea asks them to, but because they are passionate about Ikea.

Jules was searching the internet for ways to modify her beloved Ikea furniture and found all kinds of individual Ikea hacking ideas floating around. Lots and LOTS of rabid Ikea fans all over the world were talking about how they'd modified or enhanced Ikea products, but they weren't all talking to each other, and there was no one single gathering place for them to share ideas.

In about three seconds, Jules realized that she could be the one to provide that gathering place. She built www.IkeaHackers.net and it quickly became "a community of crazy IKEA fans." Community members post their best Ikea furniture hacks, shop a secondary market of Ikea stuff that's already been hacked, get project help from other hackers, and connect with each other at the IkeaHackers forum.

Jules saw individuals with the implied needs of Belonging, Recognition and Safety and she delivered the organizational structure to fill those needs. She specifically chose the domain www.IKEAHackers.com—with an "s"—because she is committed to the idea of community. To that end, the site offers up multiple connection points, from discussions that happen about a particular hack, to shoppers connecting with hackers selling their wares, to links to IkeaHacker communities on Twitter, Facebook and Google+.

A "Quick Start Guide" helps new hackers feel supported as they navigate the site. Plus there is a specific IKEAHackers forum at Ikeafans.com to lend an extra level of support and connection. Jules lays out specific steps and guidelines for submitting hacks, giving everyone a predictable process to follow. With Connection, Support and Predictability firmly in place, Ikea hackers have shown up in droves, delighted to have a community created just for them.

(As a side note, Ikea is fully aware of Ikea Hackers. They could be difficult about it and send Jules a Cease and Desist letter. But they are much savvier and smarter than that. They know that by allowing communities like Ikea Hackers to exist, they are fueling their already fiercely loyal fan base. Just another reason that this Swedish company is so incredibly successful.)

Fiercely Loyal communities can be initiated by fans like Jules or activists like Greg. With the right approach and the right tools, businesses, non-profits and other organizations can successfully create them, too.

My friend Carol Roth, author of the *New York Times* best-selling book, ***The Entrepreneur Equation,*** and regular contributor to MSNBC, Fox News, and CNN, worked with Integrity Toys, a high-end fashion doll company, to create a wildly successful community of doll collectors called The W Club (http://www.integritytoys. com/page/w_club).

An avid fashion doll enthusiast herself, Carol is personally active in the incredibly large and vibrant doll-collecting community. From this unique vantage point, she saw and heard a need specifically expressed by those who collected dolls made by Integrity Toys. They wanted a community of their own.

Being the savvy business expert that Carol is, she pitched the idea for a collector's community to Integrity Toys. She envisioned an exclusive gathering place for Integrity Toys collectors, offering connection points to the company and other collectors, as well as "Club Only" access to highly desirable dolls and other perks. Integrity Toys agreed to test this paid membership model in 2005. It's now in its seventh year of adding significant revenue to the company's bottom line.

Because Carol was listening to the right conversations in the right places, she and Integrity Toys could respond to individuals who were explicitly expressing their needs by creating and delivering the organizational structure and community they were looking for.

Takeaways and Action Steps for Building Block #4:

◎ **Keep listening.** After locating individuals and conversations that are connected to your business in some way, listen, listen, listen to the interests, wants and needs they are expressing that could be fulfilled by a community. (Yes. I know I said it before, but I cannot overemphasize how important this is.) Are they explicitly expressing a need, like Integrity Toys collectors? Or is the need more subtly implied, yet equally strong, like Ikea Hackers?

◎ **Determine if, when, where, and how your brand wants to deliver this structure and provide a community for these individuals.**

Do you need to start the community from scratch, like the Surfrider Foundation did when it created local chapters? Or are there communities already in existence that your business or organization can bring together and support in a similar way to Harley Davidson's approach?

◎ **Decide who will be the point person for your community.** Remember, success depends on an organization-wide, integrated approach. To make that work, there must be a quarterback, the person who ultimately makes the decisions and is the primary connection point to your organization. For Ikea Hackers, the quarterback is clearly Jules. She sets the tone, decides what hacks get posted, and serves as the public face for the community.

◎ **Involve members as much as you can in developing the structure of the community.** When I began building Escaping Mediocrity, I had some loose ideas on the structure I wanted to put in place. But because I wanted to create a real community, one that could function whether I was present or not, I encouraged people to take ownership of how the community operated. And they did. This collective ownership is still central to how the community functions today.

◎ **As tempting as it is, resist the "if we build it, they will come" mindset.** Many communities fail because an organization builds the structure first and then tries to locate people to join. One of the reasons The W Club and Ikea Hackers are so successful is they were created in response to obvious but unmet needs.

Building Block #5: Advanced Evolution

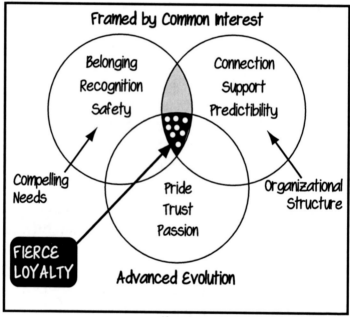

(fig. 6)

Many companies and organizations work long and hard to get a solid community up and running. They are thrilled that an inspiring frame is in place, conversations and connections are happening, that members feel supported and that there is synergy and predictability to the whole operation. After all, creating solid, on-going community is challenging and experiencing success can feel like quite an accomplishment. In fact, it feels like such an achievement that many organizations choose to settle in here, content with what they have.

Organizations in pursuit of Fierce Loyalty, however, aren't interested in just being content. They know that to reap the rewards of a wildly successful, Fiercely Loyal Community, (the five ROIs we talked about in Part 1), they must continue to grow and evolve (fig. 6). What's more, their evolutionary path can't be accidental or a random after-thought; it must be specific and intentional.

These organizations commit their time, energy, and resources to fostering three hallmark qualities that move a group from just a community to a Fiercely Loyal Community:

~ **The Evolution of Pride**. Members gain pleasure and satisfaction from their participation in their community. Community membership is a part of their identity and they are anxious to display their loyalty via t-shirts, bumper stickers, online badges, and other identifiers.

~ **The Evolution of Trust**. Members are confident that their community has their best interests at heart. A spirit of mutual reliance, faith and transparency dominates the community culture.

~ **The Evolution of Passion**. Members are deeply connected to each other and to the community as a whole. A fully developed community mission and vision spark conversation and action.

When Jules designed the IKEA Hackers community, she built several elements into the structure that naturally foster Pride, Trust and Passion. Members of the community generate the featured content by submitting their hacks. They get to take pride in having their work displayed to the rest of the community and to all site visitors. Because Jules personally screens and selects the hacks that are posted, members feel a great deal of trust in the quality and validity of the hacks, and that translates into trust in the community. And just by the very nature of the community, IKEA Hackers are passionate about the community mission.

Similarly, Carol Roth and Integrity Toys built The W Club from the beginning so that members would trust the club and the brand, take pride in all of the extra special perks that come with being a member, and develop an even deeper passion for Integrity Toys and their exclusive line of fashion dolls. All of this adds up to an incredibly profitable and wildly popular community. The W Club membership only opens for a very short window of time in January of each year. According to Carol, memberships sell fast and furiously from opening to closing bell.

case study snapshot:
TED
www.TED.com

In its early days, TED (which stands for Technology, Entertainment and Design) was a small community that gathered annually and its meetings were cloaked in secrecy. In fact, participants had to sign non-disclosure agreements promising not to reveal who was there and what was discussed.

When Chris Andersen became TED Curator, he realized that there were many people craving to belong to a community that held high-end conversations like TED, who would love a chance to be seen and heard in this community and who wanted the safety, security, and comfort of a group of like-minded people. He completely re-tooled the TED community to meet these needs.

The structure he put in place includes multiple connection points that bring together as many of these people as possible. He created an online community, a predictable system for applying to attend or speak at TED, and developed extensive avenues of support for the community as it spread the ideas discussed at the annual

TED conference. Because of this shift from a closed community to an open one, an international community sprang up around TED and its theme of "ideas worth spreading."

Under Andersen's leadership, this community continues to grow and evolve. By developing a wide variety of innovative programs like TEDx, TEDGlobal, TEDSalon, and the online TED-Community, fans have multiple opportunities to deepen their connection to TED and to other members of the TED community. These deeper connections combined with opportunities to be actively involved with the TED movement foster the growth of Pride, Trust and Passion among TED devotees.

◎

Takeaways and Action Steps for Building Block #5:

◎ **Commit the time and resources necessary to foster the advanced evolution that will move your community into Fierce Loyalty.** This evolution is a long-term commitment, not a flash-in-the-pan marketing campaign. Elevate your entire community program by mapping out a project management plan that guides the evolutionary process, complete with a budget, timelines, and staffing plans.

Creating the Fiercely Loyal community we envisioned for Hands on Memphis required a substantial commitment from our group of founders (who all had day jobs, by the way). We could have coasted on our initial success but chose to step up our frequent, regular meetings so that we could develop and implement our detailed plan that would take us where we wanted to go

Our plan included timelines, fundraising plans, and individual project assignments to establish a clear understanding of who was going to do what when. Going this extra mile transformed us from just another volunteer organization to the volunteer organization of choice, comprised of fiercely loyal members who made an incredible difference to our city.

◎ **Create intentional time and space to listen to your community.** Consider scheduling "open discussion" sessions or online chats where you put forth a topic and members do most of the talking. Listening intently to the members of The W Club allows Carol Roth and Integrity Toys to tweak the organizational structure so that it meets members' needs and to develop the right offerings that promote the development of Pride, Trust, and Passion.

◎ **Create online and/or offline experiences for members that are specifically designed to increase feelings of Pride, Trust, and**

Passion. Chris Anderson and TED do this by offering multiple opportunities and methods to be involved with TED. From viewing and discussing a TEDTalk video to participating in the online TED Community to curating a TEDx event, TED fans are encouraged to see themselves as vital and integral participants in the TED movement.

◎ **Highlight community members and allow them to contribute content to in-person and/or online gatherings.** This is the centerpiece of IKEA Hackers' success. Featuring the "hacks" submitted by members puts them in the spotlight and makes it clear that the community is about them.

◎ **Encourage self-governance and group accountability as much as is practical.** From the students at St. Louis University, to the surfers of Surfrider, to the curators of TEDx events, empowering and trusting members translates into members empowering and trusting the community. Once members take this kind ownership stake in their community, feelings of Pride, Trust, and Passion naturally follow.

part 3

Fierce Loyalty Accelerators

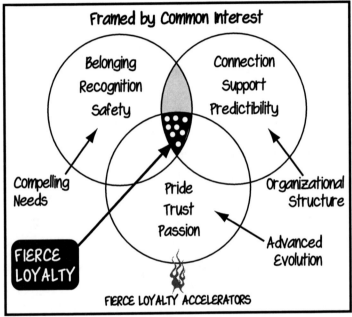

(fig. 7)

As I said earlier, it takes time for Pride, Trust and Passion to evolve and for Fierce Loyalty to develop. However, as you've gathered from the communities I've used as case studies, there are very definite "accelerators" that can turn up the heat on the evolutionary process (fig. 7). My Eleven Accelerators are not difficult and are available to anyone leading a community.

You can incorporate these accelerators at any point. I've seen really smart and successful organizations put them into action as they build the structure for their community. I've also seen organizations roll them out after their structure was in place and while they were moving toward Advanced Evolution. No matter where you are in you Fierce Loyalty journey, using these accelerators will help you get where you want to go much faster.

Eleven Fierce Loyalty Accelerators

1} Make members feel valued and important.

You can tell members of your community that they are valued and important or you can show them. The first option is easy and can ring hollow. The second option requires focused effort but the payoffs are well worth it.

In the Escaping Mediocrity community, I often say that I just hold the space for the community to gather. And I mean that. I ask for their thoughts and opinions and often highlight what they have to say in blog posts. I respond to almost every comment and carry the conversations started there into other social media channels. I empower them to take part in running the community. In fact, I know that when a trouble-maker shows up, members of the community will handle the situation more swiftly and decisively than I can. They know that Escaping Mediocrity belongs to them, and I wouldn't have it any other way.

2} Create something together.

Creating something together ignites the collective energies and talents of a community. People laugh, play and get to know each. That deep engagement, along with having a tangible finished product, builds Pride, Trust and Passion.

Samuel Adams put this accelerator into action beautifully with its Crowd-Craft Project. By collaborating on the recipe for a beer that would be brewed and available to the public, community members felt an ownership not only in the process but also in the success of their creation. Samuel Adams smartly tapped into the Passion of hand-crafted beer connoisseurs, built Trust by giving members an equal say in the final recipe, and infused the community with the Pride of "owning" the beer they collectively created.

3} Fight a common enemy.

There are no stronger bonds than those forged on the battlefield. Facing a common foe, fighting side by side and celebrating victory or tasting defeat—all draw a group together and form emotional ties that are difficult to break.

Much of Surfrider's success is based on the passion surfers feel for their favorite surfing spots. By creating an organization that channels that passion into fighting the environmental dangers that could destroy them, Surfrider gives all of its members a common target, no matter where they are in the world. When one chapter scores a victory against the common enemy, every chapter celebrates. As the community fights together and celebrates victories together, members feel more Pride in the work they do, more Trust in each member and each chapter to do their part, and more Passion to keep the fight going.

4} Create a culture of "We."

Traditionally, the relationship between an organization and its clients is based on an "us" and "them" paradigm. Over and over again, I hear "those clients," "those customers" and "those donors." What if we eliminated the whole idea of "us and them"? What if there was only "we"?

No one does this better than Harley-Davidson. Just one glimpse at the Harley-Davidson website reveals that this isn't "corporate" talking to "customers." This is Harley owners who just happen to work at the corporate office talking with other Harley owners who don't. By creating community "with" their customers, rather than "for" their customers, Harley Davidson eliminates that traditional "us and them" mentality that pervades most company/customer relationships, and creates a culture of "we."

5} Empower members to make the community their own.

We are fiercely loyal to those people, places, and things that we can call our own. They are a part of who we are, a piece of our identity. Relinquish control, give members an ownership stake, and watch Fierce Loyalty soar.

Allowing students in a residence hall to run their community with minimal input from "the adults" was a huge shift in traditional residence hall management. They chose their own paint designs, set up and enforced their own rules, determined how to spend their allocated hall budgets and more. They were given some guidance of course, but in the end, the decision-making belonged to them. Predictable (but not terminal) disasters came to pass, and incredible successes were celebrated. This community ownership drove student Pride, Trust, and Passion, and was the reason the whole concept succeeded.

6} Build in exclusivity.

Let's face it. We all like the feeling of belonging to something that is exclusively for us and people like us. Customers and clients who belong to an exclusive community know beyond a shadow of a doubt that it will deliver value that is specifically designed for their interests and their needs.

Running Room is very clear and specific about the members of their community: they are exclusively runners. They are not cyclists. They are not weight lifters. They are not yoga enthusiasts. Clearly delineating who Running Room is for makes it very easy for runners to know they belong there and that they won't be mixed into a general group of fitness enthusiasts. The community can speak specifically to runners and tap into their unique motivators for Pride, Trust, and Passion.

7} Create a barrier to entry.

A barrier to entry is an extra requirement, an extra hurdle individuals must jump over to belong to the community. Demonstrating this serious commitment to the community and knowing everyone in the group leapt the same hurdle instantly amps up the Fierce Loyalty factor.

While "The W Club" is exclusively for collectors of Integrity Toys, these collectors must pass through a barrier to enter the community and become members. That barrier is a membership fee. Requiring this extra level of commitment ensures that the community is composed of passionate, serious collectors, firmly committed to the community. Members are confident that the peer group gathering at The W Club share the same level of Passion, lending immediate Pride and Trust to the community.

8} Stand for something bold.

Taking a bold stand not only allows you to rise above all the noise in today's marketplace but also to attract a very distinct group of customers who want to be associated specifically with you and your organization.

There are lots of international conferences these days, but none have a Fiercely Loyal Community like the TED community. TED's bold identity centers on creating access to cutting-edge thinkers and ideas not found anywhere else. This bold stand communicates exactly what TED is and is not, and attracts a very distinct group of people who strongly identify with TED's mission. Belonging to, participating in, and being identified with something bold ramps up levels of Pride, Trust and Passion.

9} Build organizational structure with an eye toward fostering Pride, Trust, and Passion.

It's never too early to start thinking about and planning for your community's evolution to Fierce Loyalty. As you build or tweak the organizational structure for your community, build in opportunities that will encourage feelings of Pride, Trust, and Passion among members.

Jules built the organizational structure for IKEA Hackers so that it provides Connection, Support, and Predictability for this specific group of enthusiasts, and encourages Pride, Trust, and Passion at the same time. Site content centers around "hacks" created by members. Jules vets all hack submissions and selects those that are posted. Every feature of the site is designed to feed the passion of this "community of crazy IKEA fans."

10} Initiate opportunities for shared experiences.

Shared experiences allow a community to build a common bond, a common history, a common "story," even a common vocabulary. Initiate experiences—both online and in person—that everyone in your community can take part in. Pride, Trust and Passion will take root and flourish.

Hands on Memphis built its entire volunteer community model around creating shared experiences. By sweating through volunteer projects, hanging out at a local watering hole after a hard day's work, or making an annual citywide, all-day volunteer event happen, members forged close relationships as well as a common history. These relationships and this history created a strong emotional tie to Hands on Memphis and its mission, and fueled the rapid growth of Pride, Trust, and Passion in being a part of this community.

11} Love your community.

Love your community and those who are in it. I mean really really love them, not just for what they can do for you but because each member truly matters to you. Be interested in them, pay attention to them, get to know them, spend time with them, and be vulnerable with them. Aren't these the things we do with people we value?

All of the organizations I've talked about in this book excel at loving their community. Harley-Davidson loves their Harley owners. Surfrider loves their surfers. Running Room loves their runners. The interest, care and concern these groups feel for their community members is palpable in everything they do. There is no greater accelerator for Fierce Loyalty than Love.

final thoughts

Now that you have all the building blocks you need to create a Fiercely Loyal community in and around your organization, it's very tempting to jump right in and start doing. And I really want you to jump in and start doing. Before you do, though, take a deep breath here and pause. Reconnect with why you want a Fiercely Loyal community. More importantly, get centered on why people might want to be Fiercely Loyal to your community.

Earlier in this book, I told you that so many leaders I talk to view having a wildly successful, fiercely loyal community as a matter of chance or a matter of frustration. I've given you the DNA, the internal building blocks, so that you can sidestep this guessing and this aggravation. You know exactly what to do to make Fierce Loyalty a reality for your organization. You have Action Steps to guide you all along the way and accelerators to use to light a fire under you Fierce Loyalty efforts.

Have you started using the model? The action steps? The accelerators? If you have – that's awesome!! Keep your eye on the prize and stay focused on what you and your organization are accomplishing. If you haven't, what's stopping you? All the theoretical knowledge in the world won't bring you a Fiercely Loyal, wildly successful community. Taking the right actions continuously is the only way to get where you want to go. If Fierce Loyalty is what you want, commit to taking those actions, and get started right now.

To help you get the most of Fierce Loyalty, I've created a dedicated website and community at www.Fierce-Loyalty.com. You'll find blog posts, case studies, interviews, discussions, and other resources that will support your efforts and expand your knowledge. If you want more in depth training, you'll find information about current and upcoming Fierce Loyalty workshops around the country. If you'd like to explore how your organization can work directly with me on implementing Fierce Loyalty, you'll find information about that too.

I am thrilled beyond words that you've spent this time with me, mapping out your own Fiercely Loyal Community. You have so much competing for your time and your attention, so I am honored you chose to give some of these precious resources to read this e-book. I hope the model, the action steps, the ideas, and the strategies make a difference to you and your organization in the coming days, months, and years.

Human beings are born with the deep yearning to feel engaged and connected to each other. These feelings are essential to our happiness. As you build and strengthen your community and make it a place of engagement and connection, you add more happiness to another person's world. Isn't that an idea to feel fiercely loyal about every day?

Love,

Sarah

P.S. If you found this book valuable, I'd love it if you join the Fierce Loyalty community at http://www.Fierce-Loyalty.com, and I'd love your help in spreading the word about Fierce Loyalty.

Here are a few ideas on how you easily do that: Think of 1–3 colleagues who would benefit from reading this book and recommend it to them simply by copying this link—http://www.FierceLoyaltyBook—and pasting it into an email or any of your social media channels. If you have a blog, feel free to share it there as well. In fact, I've put together a Bloggers Kit and other resources to make it super simple to share Fierce Loyalty. You'll find them at http://www.FierceLoyaltyBook.com.

Thank you!

acknowledgements

This book would not exist with the help, support and encouragement of so many people I want to thank. First, Janet Goldstein and Elizabeth Marshall who helped me uncover and shape Fierce Loyalty. Your patience, your understanding and your guidance are incredible gifts to me. The Escaping Mediocrity Tribe, who teach me about Fierce Loyalty every single day. Les McKeown, whose ability to think in Venn Diagrams helped give birth to the Fierce Loyalty Model. My mom, Alice Chistenson, the best editor and proofreader on the planet. Barry Moltz, the greatest Fierce Loyalty evangelist out there. Jenny Schmitt, who believes in Fierce Loyalty as much as I do. And finally, my family—David, Thomas and Nicholas— You have my fiercest love, devotion and loyalty.

CPSIA information can be obtained at www.ICGtesting.com
Printed in the USA
LVOW10s0509210913

353432LV00003B/4/P